Oceans

Joy Palmer

RSVP

RAINTREE
STECK-VAUGHN
PUBLISHERS

The Steck-Vaughn Company

Austin, Texas

Editor: A. Patricia Sechi
Designer: Shaun Barlow
Project Manager: Joyce Spicer
Electronic Production:
    Scott Melcer
Artwork: Alex Pang
Cover artwork: Alex Pang

Educational Advisor:
    Joy Richardson
Consultant: Miranda MacQuitty

Library of Congress
Cataloging-in-Publication Data

Palmer, Joy.
    Oceans / Joy Palmer.
        p.   cm. — (What About)
    Includes index.
    Summary: Describes the world's oceans, discussing marine plants and animals, how people use the ocean's resources, and protecting oceans from pollution.
    Hardcover   ISBN 0-8114-3401-X
    Softcover   ISBN 0-8114-4915-7
    1. Ocean — Juvenile literature.
[1. Ocean.] I. Title. II. Series.
GC21.5.P35 1992
574.5'2636—dc20   92-12409
                                    CIP
                                    AC

Printed and bound in the United States

5 6 7 8 9 0 LB 00 99 98 97 96 95

Contents

What Are Oceans?

Most of the Earth is covered in water. You can look at a globe to see how much of the Earth's surface is colored blue. This water lies around the land and each large area is called an ocean. Thousands of different plants and animals live in the oceans.

▽ Oceans cover large areas of the Earth. They stretch for many thousands of miles.

Where Are Oceans?

There are four oceans, named the Pacific, the Atlantic, the Indian, and the Arctic. The Pacific is the largest ocean. It covers more of the Earth's surface than all the land put together!

The oceans contain smaller areas of water called **seas**. Land shapes partly cut off these areas from the oceans.

▷ Much of the Earth's surface is covered with water.

▽ **Beaches** are sometimes made where the oceans meet the land.

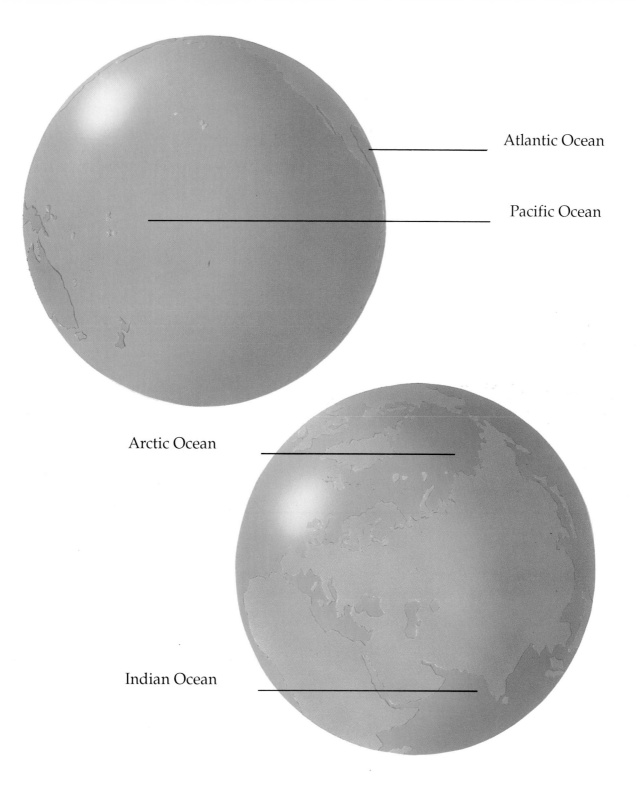

Atlantic Ocean

Pacific Ocean

Arctic Ocean

Indian Ocean

What Are Oceans Like?

If you watch the ocean for a day, you can see the water level rise and fall, as the **tide** goes in and out. The tides are made by the pull of the sun and moon on the Earth.

Seawater is salty because it contains **minerals**. As the seawater washes and wears down rocks on the shore, minerals are washed into the sea.

▷ When seawater dries in the sun, it leaves salt. Salt looks like white crystals.

▽ At low tide the sea level falls. It may be so low that it leaves the seabed showing.

▽ At high tide the sea level rises.

Are Oceans Warm or Cold?

Near the **equator**, the oceans are warm. Near the North and South Poles, the oceans are so cold that the surface freezes.

The movement of the waves carries warm or cold water to different parts of the oceans. The ocean is usually colder at deeper levels.

▷ Warm, clear seas sometimes have shallow water where many small animals live.

▽ The sea at the North Pole is frozen all year round.

Waves

The water in the world's oceans is never still. The wind makes ripples and waves. If the wind blows hard for a long time, the waves grow bigger and stronger. Sometimes the earth moves under the sea. This can set off a huge tidal wave. When tidal waves reach land, their force can kill people and destroy homes.

▷ Tidal waves are huge waves. They are very dangerous.

▽ A slight wind makes small waves called ripples.

▽ Waves can wear away the land. This can leave **cliffs** and rocks in strange shapes.

▽ Waves that
break up are called
whitecaps.

Plants

Plants that live in the oceans have to be able to survive the salt. Many seaweeds live in the oceans. They do not live in deep water because they need sunlight to survive. Land plants are stiff, but water plants can bend, so they can move with the water and not snap. Near the shore, plants grow in marshes and on the sand.

▽ Cord grass grows in marshes. It gets rid of the salt it takes in by sweating it out.

▽ Mangrove trees grow in swamps. Their large roots keep them from being washed away.

▽ Eelgrass is not a seaweed, but it is a plant that grows in the sea.

△ Many seaweeds have air-filled pockets that keep them afloat near the light.

▽ Some seaweeds are red or brown.

Fish

Fish live in all the oceans. Their smooth and tapered bodies move easily through the water. They breathe through **gills**, which take in oxygen from the water.

Fish live at different levels of the oceans. The lantern fish lives deep down and sardines live near the surface. Most fish eat smaller fish to survive.

▷ Many smaller fish live in groups or schools to protect themselves against enemies, or **predators**.

△ Tuna fish live in all oceans except the coldest ones.

△ Rays are flat fish that live on the seabed.

◁ The shape of a shark's body helps it move quickly through the ocean.

◁ Sardines are small fish that live in groups near the surface of the ocean.

▽ The lantern fish glows green to attract other fish and then catches them.

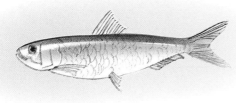

△ The flounder's color hides it from other fish that might want to eat it.

15

Fantastic Creatures

There are many strange-looking creatures living in the oceans, like the octopus and the jellyfish. Each animal is suited to the part of the ocean where it lives. Sea anemones stay in the same spot. Crabs crawl along the sea bottom where they catch their food.

▽ The sea horse is a fish. It lives among seaweeds and underwater grasses.

▷ Jellyfish are bell-shaped and have many tentacles or arms.

▽ Anemones sting animals with their many arms and then eat them.

▽ The octopus lives on the seabed. It uses its arms to catch passing animals.

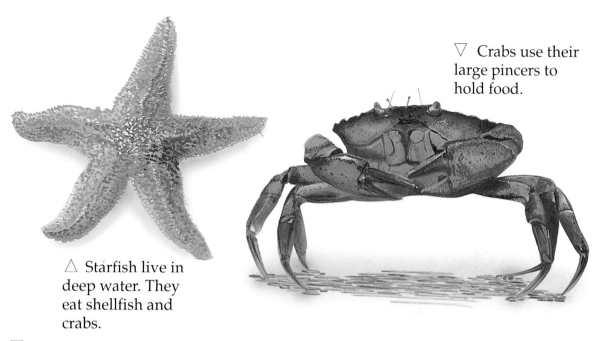

▽ Crabs use their large pincers to hold food.

△ Starfish live in deep water. They eat shellfish and crabs.

▽ Tiny creatures and plants called **plankton** live in seawater.

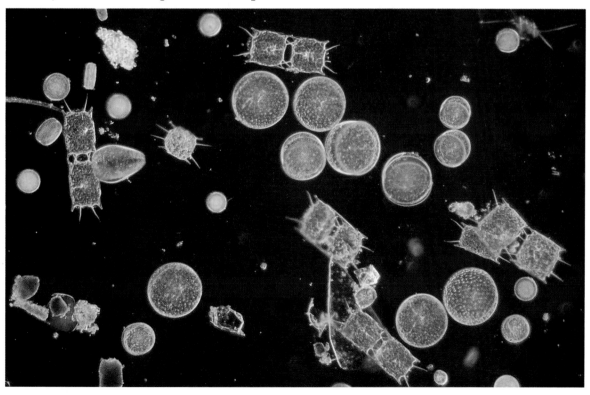

Mammals and Reptiles

Whales are the largest creatures in the sea. Whales look like fish, but they are **mammals**. Like us, they have lungs and cannot stay under water all the time. They come to the surface to breathe.

Sea snakes and turtles are **reptiles** that live in the sea. Reptiles breathe air and have scaly skins.

▽ The sea otter is a furry creature. It floats on its back while eating shellfish and crabs.

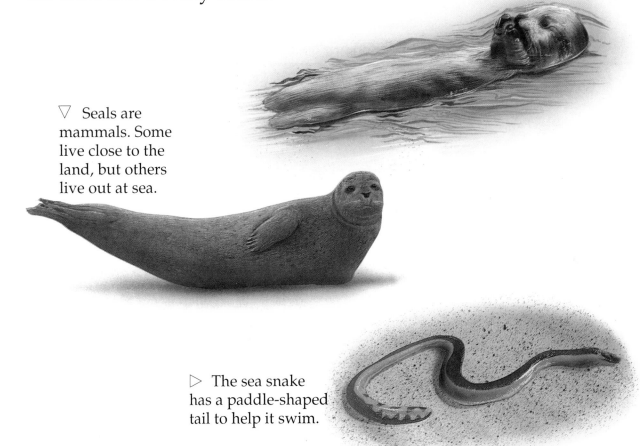

▽ Seals are mammals. Some live close to the land, but others live out at sea.

▷ The sea snake has a paddle-shaped tail to help it swim.

▷ The killer whale is easy to spot with its black-and-white markings.

▽ The shape of a dolphin's body helps it move quickly through the water.

▷ The green turtle lives in the warm oceans of the world.

Birds

Seabirds live on land near the oceans. They rely on the seas for food. Many seabirds have webbed feet and well-oiled feathers. Birds such as gulls and pelicans usually stay close to land. Penguins spend most of their lives at sea.

▽ The albatross has the largest wingspan of all seabirds.

△ Sailors know they are near land when they see gulls flying above.

◁ Puffins live near the shore and on islands in the northern oceans.

▽ Storm petrels are the smallest seabirds.

▷ Penguins are very well suited to living at sea. They only use their wings for swimming.

△ Gannets fly high above the water.

▽ The brown pelican is a seabird. Other pelicans live near fresh water.

People and the Ocean

Sometimes we only see the world's oceans when we go on vacation. Then we go swimming or sailing. Some people work on the oceans in fishing boats or on oil platforms. We use the seas like roads, too. For thousands of years, people have traveled across the seas carrying goods from country to country.

▷ In some countries seaweed is farmed for food.

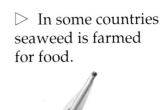

▽ Many people go sailing in small boats.

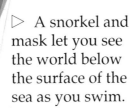

▷ A snorkel and mask let you see the world below the surface of the sea as you swim.

▽ Oil is drilled from the seabed and pumped ashore.

▽ Large ships called tankers carry oil across the oceans.

Riches from the Seas

The oceans give us food, energy, and minerals. Millions of fish are caught each year for people to eat. Fish are also used to make oil or animal feed. Power from the ocean waves is used to make electricity in some countries. We gather salt from the sea. And we use coral and pearls in jewelry.

▽ Salt is gathered from pans where it is left behind when seawater dries up.

▽ Sponges are the skeletons of sea creatures.

◁ Coral is a mass of tubes made for shelter by tiny animals. It is made into jewelry.

▷ This power station makes electricity from the rise and fall of the waves.

▽ Pearls are found in shellfish called oysters. Pearls are like small beads.

▽ Fishing boats catch fish by using large nets.

Threats to the Oceans

We use the sea, but we must learn to protect it. Some types of fish will die out if we do not catch fewer fish each year. Visitors to beaches leave litter behind. It may harm animals, which can become caught in plastic wrappings. Waste is dumped at sea, **polluting** the water and killing animals.

▷ Oil spills kill many sea animals, which swallow the oil or become coated in it.

▽ Overfishing reduces the numbers of fish and some types could die out altogether.

▷ Litter spoils beaches and can be dangerous.

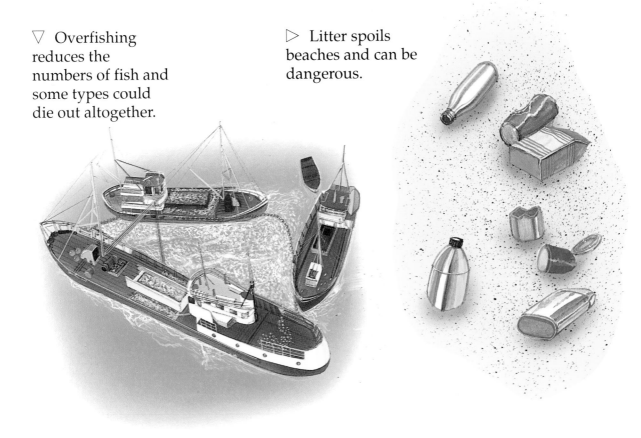

▽ Factories dump
waste chemicals
into the sea.

Ocean Dangers

Safety at sea is important. People who go sailing wear life jackets in case they fall overboard. Lighthouses warn sailors of rocks. Lighted buoys mark where ships can sail safely. If a boat is in trouble at sea, lifeboats are sent out. On the beach, lifeguards watch for swimmers who may need help.

▽ A lighthouse has a light that can be seen far out to sea to warn ships of danger.

△ This life jacket is an inflatable vest that keeps you afloat.

◁ Lifeguards keep watch on the shore for people who may need help.

◁ Lighted buoys are small floating lights that mark safe routes.

▽ Lifeboats are launched to rescue people in trouble at sea.

Things to Do

- When you visit the seashore, collect the shells of sea creatures. Only collect the shells if there is no creature inside.

- Collect pebbles or pieces of wood from the beach. Look to see how the waves have shaped and smoothed them.

- Look through a magnifying glass at a handful of sand. What can you find? You may be able to see bits of shell and rock. What color are they?

Useful Addresses:

Atlantic Center for the
    Environment
39 South Main Street
Ipswich, Mass. 09138-2321

Barrier Island Coalition
122 East 42nd Street, Suite 4500
New York, NY 10168

Center for Marine Conservation
1725 De Sales, N.W., Suite 500
Washington, DC 20036

Friends of the Earth
530 Seventh Street, S.E.
Washington, DC 20003

Greenpeace
1611 Connecticut Avenue
Washington, DC 20009

National Coalition for Marine
    Conservation
P.O. Box 23298
Savannah, GA 31403

Glossary

beach   A strip of land at the edge of the sea, made out of rocks and shells left behind by the waves.

cliffs   Steep rocks that stand high over the sea and extend down into the water.

equator   The equator is an imaginary line around the middle of the Earth.

gills   Comb-like organs that fish use to absorb oxygen from the water.

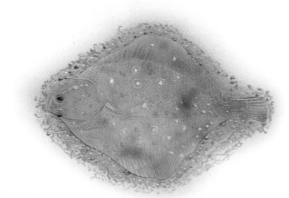

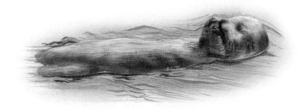

mammal   An animal that has hair, gives birth to its young, and feeds them with milk.

mineral   A substance that is not alive and can be dug out of the ground. Coal, gold, and diamonds are examples of minerals.

plankton   Microscopic animals and plants that live in the oceans.

pollution   Spoiling the oceans, land, and air by dumping wastes and other harmful substances.

predator   An animal that kills and eats other animals.

reptile   An animal that has a scaly skin and that lays eggs, like a snake or a lizard.

sea   The bodies of salty water that cover much of the Earth.

tide   The rise and fall of the sea each day. It is caused by the pull of the moon and the sun on the Earth.

Index

Photographic credits: Bruce Coleman 23, (C. B. & D. W. Frith) 9, (Dr. Eckart Pott) 13, 21, (Bill Wood) cover, 15; Robert Harding 29, (David Lomax) 25; Eric and David Hosking (D. P. Wilson) 17; Frank Lane Picture Agency cover, 4; N.H.P.A. (David Woodfall) 27; Survival Anglia (Dieter and Mary Plage) 11; Zefa 3.